TO MIND YOUR LIFE

TO MIND YOUR LIFE

POEMS FOR NURSES AND MIDWIVES

Edited by
Dr Marti Balaam
Samuel Tongue
with
Prof Clare Cable
Dr Kath MacDonald
Dr Jenny Patterson
Tasha Prigmore
Prof John Gillies

Scottish **Poetry** Library

Polygon

First published in paperback in 2021 by the Scottish Poetry Library
5 Crichton's Close, Edinburgh EH8 8DT and
Polygon, an imprint of Birlinn Ltd
West Newington House, 10 Newington Road
Edinbrugh EH9 1QS

9 8 7 6 5 4 3 2 1

www.scottishpoetrylibrary.org.uk
www.polygonbooks.co.uk

ISBN 978 1 84697 587 5

Typeset in Verdigris MVB by Polygon, Edinburgh
Cover design by Polygon, based on the original series design by
Gerry Cambridge.

The publishers are grateful for partner support towards
the costs of this anthology.

CONTENTS

III. SETTING OUT

The path of hope

IV. GRIT AND GRACE
Making sense of pain and death

V. STILL WE RISE
Finding our voices and being the change

FROM THE EDITORS

Many congratulations on becoming a nurse or a midwife. Whether you graduated recently or many years ago, becoming a nurse or a midwife is a wonderful achievement. Sharing other people's lives, often when they are at their most vulnerable, is a privilege. However, the compassion we provide to others is often difficult to find for ourselves. Midwives and nurses are well-known for battling on in stressful situations and not attending to their own wellbeing. And yet, compassion and self-care are vital in order for us to care for others and for our communities. We hope that *To Mind Your Life* will give you permission to pause, reflect, and recharge.

To Mind Your Life is a gift to you, a friend to accompany and comfort you through your journey, in whatever form that takes. These poems demonstrate compassion for ourselves and others, in the patient-carer relationship, and in the stories of what it means to be a midwife or nurse. We also present visions of hope, kindness, and inspiration within these pages, all of which are powerful antidotes to the many challenges that we face together.

The book is divided into five sections which reflect important aspects of our human journey. We begin with Kindness for ourselves and others, focussing on compassion as the ideal heart of every encounter. We then move on to Self-Care, often overlooked in busy days and lives but fundamental to our wellbeing. Next, we offer poems that reflect on Setting Out, charting paths of hope through adversity; it is through our darkest times that we need glimpses of light. Grit and Grace is honest about some of the hard times and situations that are part of every caring career, but Still We Rise, adapted from the famous poem of Maya Angelou, ends with an inspiring call to action: no matter how low we may fall (or are pushed) we always have the ability to overcome difficult situations. Throughout our selection process, we kept these titles in mind, and collated poems that we hope speak directly to your experiences, or communicate something more to help interpret those experiences.

We are grateful to the Queen's Nursing Institute Scotland (QNIS), the Royal College of Midwives (RCM), and the Medical and Dental Defence Union of Scotland (MDDUS) for their generous support for this first edition of *To Mind Your Life: Poems for Nurses and Midwives*, and to the Scottish Poetry Library for their expertise in bringing this project to fruition. Thanks also to Polygon for adding this book to the series for health and wellbeing, 'Pocket Poetry', where it joins sister publications *Tools of the Trade: Poems for New Doctors* and *To Learn the Future: Poems for Teachers*. We are also grateful to Marcas Mac an Tuairneir for assistance with sourcing Gaelic poems. Kind thanks to all of our supporters who took the time to provide feedback and quotes to help publicise our work.

We believe that engaging with poetry gives us a place of emotional respite and release; it can gently comfort and encourage us and can resonate with many of the human experiences and dilemmas we all face. So carry this book in your pocket, keep it by your side, and let the voices of others inspire you as you walk. In the words of the poet Miroslav Holub, 'Go and open the door . . .'

Dr Marti Balaam
Samuel Tongue
Prof Clare Cable
Dr Kath MacDonald
Dr Jenny Patterson
Tasha Prigmore
Prof John Gillies

PREFACE: QUEEN'S NURSING
INSTITUTE SCOTLAND

This anthology has been curated to accompany your journey as a nurse or a midwife, whether you are setting out or in need of comfort, inspiration, and encouragement along the way. This little book is filled with words of wisdom, and I hope you will find poems that resonate in different times over the months and years to come.

Nursing and midwifery are both science and art. Contained within this volume you will find words that speak to the complexity and alchemy at the heart of our professions. This collection does not shy away from the challenges, offering a range of perspectives, expressing the pain and frustration in ways that make us feel less alone.

These poems speak of connection, compassion, and deep listening – to self and others. In an already busy, sometimes stressful, working life we rarely give ourselves the time to slow down. I truly believe that without this space to reflect we deny ourselves the opportunity to grow and transform. These poems invite us to step away from doing and step into being, to pause and be still. It is when we stop to take breath that we can become truly present, and make a difference one conversation at a time.

This volume was brought together during 2020 – the year of the nurse and midwife, but also the first long year of COVID-19. It has brought into sharp relief our need for courageous and compassionate healthcare professionals. The Queen's Nursing Institute Scotland is delighted to have been able to fund and contribute editorially to the production of *To Mind Your Life: Poems for Nurses and Midwives*, a pocket-sized book that encapsulates what it means to bring knowledge, skill, and kindness to being a professional.

Professor Clare Cable
Chief Executive and
Nurse Director
Queen's Nursing Institute
Scotland

PREFACE: ROYAL COLLEGE OF MIDWIVES, SCOTLAND

The Royal College of Midwives in Scotland is delighted to have been able to support the publication of this book of poems for newly qualified nurses and midwives.

As a midwife, you will be privileged to witness some of the most life-changing moments of a person's life. You will be there to support women and families during times of huge joy, but also times of pain, worry, and loss.

What I love about this book is that it gives you a way to stop, to reflect and to remember why you chose this path. The joy of a poem is, I think, partly that it is short enough to be read before you fall asleep after an exhausting night shift, but also that a poem can be a beautiful shot of light – reminding us about what really matters. Here, the poems focus on kindness, compassion, learning from hardship, caring for yourself – these are all absolutely central to being a good midwife.

The book includes two of my favourite poems – 'Welcome Wee One' is the poem by Jackie Kay that is included in the baby box that every baby born in Scotland receives; and 'Still I Rise' by Maya Angelou is a poem that has accompanied me throughout my life, to remind me I am strong. I hope that you will find at least one poem that can accompany you through life, reminding you of your core values.

I hope that this book will be something that you can return to – when you are tired, when you are not sure that you can carry on, when you feel you have lost sight of why you chose this life, this career, this vocation of midwifery. These poems will remind you to take five minutes for yourself, go outside, look at the sea, the trees, and breathe.

Dr Mary Ross-Davie
Director
Royal College of Midwives,
Scotland

INTRODUCTION

Years ago, I had a job as a cleaner in a hospital. Sometimes I cleaned out the morgue – I'd always say hello to the corpse, I couldn't bear the idea of the body of a person being in the room and them not getting the courtesy of a hello; I raked the gardens too. Once, a friend saw me and laughed at how little my interest in poetry had gotten me. I'd triple clean rooms of infection, and I hate the smell of Jif to this day. And I'd clean the operating theatres, too. The nurse in charge of the operating corridor scoffed at me when I asked her what kind of a doctor she was. *A doctor couldn't run this place*, she said before teaching me how not to gag when cleaning up blood.

In the drama of an operating theatre, I saw much humanity. I saw a frightened nun shaking with fear before an operation once. The nurse called me over and said, *Talk to her, she needs the sound of a voice.* Another time, a patient was distressed by the nonchalance of an intimate examination. The nurse intervened, offered a conversation about an ordinary thing while an unordinary thing was happening elsewhere on the body. Once, a patient was anxious about having a catheter put in. Anxious and shy and ashamed. The nurse made a joke, everyone laughed, the nurse could finish the job, and the patient seemed to trust the room a little more, too, after that.

Nursing and midwifery are jobs of extraordinary skill: science, symptoms, wellbeing, flourishing, vitals, nurture, signs of healing, signs of concern. And amidst all of this, too, is that unteachable thing that can support a person, whether in a ward for a procedure, a scare, a birth, a death, a shock, a test, a result. I've seen midwives and nurses take a reading of a moment of anxiety and use their voice to create something new in an otherwise panicked room. It might be a small consolation. It might be a compliment. It might be a supportive touch, or a reminder to breathe. It might be an intervention with clear fact when fantasised fear threatens to overwhelm.

What do you call such moments? I call them poems. A poem is a created thing; a thing created out of nothing but possibility, language, air, and need. Midwives and nurses rarely tell patients that they love them – even when they do. But the hope of these demanding jobs is that patients feel loved enough in whatever they're facing: a new phase of life, an adjustment, a joy, a grief, an end. Someone felt like their only name was sorrow, once, and wrote a poem about it, naming in a poem what their life needed: Sorrow is not my name, Ross Gay writes. Someone was under huge demand once, and realised that ironic thing – if you stand very still, you might find the strength that stress is stealing from you. We thank Patience Strong for her strength. Roger

Robinson watches a nurse and marvels at the capacity for skill, science, care, efficiency, and instinct he sees. He wonders about the hands of nurses, washed so often the skin peels. Colin MacDuff looks at the body of his father, dead just an hour, and takes the watch off his dad's wrist before washing him. Alongside him is someone who has spent years studying and practising. In grit and grace, with no spin, he is brought into what nursing and midwifing in the face of life and death might look like; and he's sold. And Jackie Kay sings a lullaby to living, in honour of all babies, births, mothers, and midwives. I never kent love like this.

We all need created things to help us face the day. Whether in a crisis ourselves, or helping someone face theirs. Whether facing the delight of life, or the shock at it. We need skilled hands, focused minds, and the kind of words that can conjure kindness and sense out of chaos, and senselessness. For this, we have midwives and nurses. And for you – people whose lives and bodies we rely on – we offer poems of thanks and honour.

Pádraig Ó Tuama
*Irish poet and theologian, and
presenter of* Poetry Unbound
from On Being *Studios.*

I. KINDNESS

Compassion at the heart of every encounter

*

KINDNESS

All that matters is kindness
I know it sounds obvious
But it's true
Think of all the bad things in the world
And then think of you
Thing about all the troubles you've faced
And then think of all the kind faces
That pulled you through
It's them that reminded
You of your power
And on those days you feel you've got little purpose
Remember as humans it's as basic as showering
Others with kindness
Compassion
Lashings
Of love
Regardless of race, sex, location, and material stuff
It's kindness in its simplest sense
That will take us from this dark present
Into a more hopeful, prospecting tense

Charly Cox

THE ORANGE

At lunchtime I bought a huge orange
The size of it made us all laugh.
I peeled it and shared it with Robert and Dave—
They got quarters and I had a half.

And that orange it made me so happy,
As ordinary things often do
Just lately. The shopping. A walk in the park
This is peace and contentment. It's new.

The rest of the day was quite easy.
I did all my jobs on my list
And enjoyed them and had some time over.
I love you. I'm glad I exist.

Wendy Cope

THE GUEST HOUSE

This being human is a guest house.
Every morning a new arrival.

A joy, a depression, a meanness,
some momentary awareness comes
as an unexpected visitor.

Welcome and entertain them all!
Even if they're a crowd of sorrows,
who violently sweep your house
empty of its furniture,
still, treat each guest honorably.
He may be clearing you out
for some new delight.

The dark thought, the shame, the malice,
meet them at the door laughing,
and invite them in.

Be grateful for whoever comes,
because each has been sent
as a guide from beyond.

Jelaluddin Rumi
Translated by Coleman Barks

CARING

Caring is loving, motionless,
An interval of more and less
Between the stress and the distress.

After the present falls the past,
After the festival, the fast.
Always the deepest is the last.

This is the circle we must trace,
Not spiralled outward, but a space
Returning to its starting place.

Centre of all we mourn and bless,
Centre of calm beyond excess,
Who cares for caring, has caress.

F. R. Scott

NIGHTINGALE PLEDGE

Before God and those assembled here, I pledge:
I will check the screen tracing your heart rhythm –
the beep steady as a bird's call from the shadows.
I will tie your gown, so faithfully strong
it won't show your bare back, your leaf-like keloid.
Only filtered air will stroke your unwashed hair.
I will carry out to the best of my ability
my nocturnal duties – the warm Horlicks,
the call bell, the ajar door. I will devote
my midnight listening to you hum a song –
something that lessens the weight of my eyelids.
I will attend to the sound of your bare feet
as they touch the sticky floor. In the morning
I will explain what the cylindrical bottles are for;
without a word, you'll unbend your arm to me.
My fingertip will search for the strongest vein.
I will not do anything evil. The defib pads
will fly out of the metal drawer, I will slap them
on your chest: one on the right, below the clavicle,
the other on the left, just under the armpit.
I will be the first one to greet you, Welcome back.
Even if I know you'd rather go. I will not reveal
the story of your life, how your daughter left
when she learned of your diagnosis.
I will devote my hours listening to things

you do not say. I will maintain the prestige
of my profession, but release a wild laugh
when I find you pretend choking
on your egg-white tablets
so I will pat your back.

Romalyn Ante

SORROW IS NOT MY NAME

– after Gwendolyn Brooks

No matter the pull toward brink. No
matter the florid, deep sleep awaits.
There is a time for everything. Look,
just this morning a vulture
nodded his red, grizzled head at me,
and I looked at him, admiring
the sickle of his beak.
Then the wind kicked up, and,
after arranging that good suit of feathers
he up and took off.
Just like that. And to boot,
there are, on this planet alone, something like two
million naturally occurring sweet things,
some with names so generous as to kick
the steel from my knees: agave, persimmon,
stick ball, the purple okra I bought for two bucks
at the market. Think of that. The long night,
the skeleton in the mirror, the man behind me
on the bus taking notes, yeah, yeah.

But look; my niece is running through a field
calling my name. My neighbor sings like an angel
and at the end of my block is a basketball court.
I remember. My color's green. I'm spring.

– for Walter Aikens

Ross Gay

II. SELF-CARE

Your own oxygen mask first

*

THE PEACE OF WILD THINGS

When despair for the world grows in me
and I wake in the night at the least sound
in fear of what my life and my children's lives may be,
I go and lie down where the wood drake
rests in his beauty on the water, and the great heron feeds.
I come into the peace of wild things
who do not tax their lives with forethought
of grief. I come into the presence of still water.
And I feel above me the day-blind stars
waiting with their light. For a time
I rest in the grace of the world, and am free.

Wendell Berry

THIS IS THE TIME TO BE SLOW

This is the time to be slow,
Lie low to the wall
Until the bitter weather passes.
Try, as best you can, not to let
The wire brush of doubt
Scrape from your heart
All sense of yourself
And your hesitant light.

If you remain generous,
Time will come good;
And you will find your feet
Again on fresh pastures of promise,
Where the air will be kind
And blushed with beginning.

John O'Donohue

FAITH

Keep faith wi life.
And dinna ging back on fit ye aince believed
Haud fast yer dreams
Had heech yer hopes
An dinna be deceived.
Dinna betray the great ideals
Wi fit ye jist set oot.
Had on tay youth's sweet promises
Haud on an nivver doot
Be true tay a' that ee hiv hoped.
Pursue the happy quest.
Keep faith wi life and life at last
Will gee ye o' its best.

Adeline Smith Reid

IF ONCE YOU HAVE SLEPT ON AN ISLAND

If once you have slept on an island
You'll never be quite the same;
You may look as you looked the day before
And go by the same old name,
You may bustle about in street and shop
You may sit at home and sew,
But you'll see blue water and wheeling gulls
Wherever your feet may go.
You may chat with the neighbors of this and that
And close to your fire keep,
But you'll hear ship whistle and lighthouse bell
And tides beat through your sleep.
Oh! you won't know why and you can't say how
Such a change upon you came,
But once you have slept on an island,
You'll never be quite the same.

Rachel Lyman Field

REST
for Carol Ann Duffy

I expect you might at some point tonight
Beneath the sheets before sleep
Still reeling from the flaying lights,
Want or more likely seek

Rest. There is no manifesto in this
Nor snake-like list of things to do.
There is no tomorrow either,
There's poetry as ever and you.

                              Lemn Sissay

IF YOU STAND VERY STILL

If you stand very still in the heart of a wood
You will hear many wonderful things.
The snap of a twig and the wind in the trees
And the whirl of invisible wings.

If you stand very still in the turmoil of life
And you wait for the voice from within,
You'll be led down the way of wisdom and peace,
Through the rough world of chaos and din.

If you stand very still and hold onto your faith
You'll get all the help that you ask.
You will draw from the silence the things that you need –
Hope and courage and strength for your task.

Patience Strong

ALL AROUND US

An ever-changing world
So important to believe,
In that small word with huge meaning
That will get us through.

Listen closely, you can hear it,
In those kind comforting words,
Be mindful and feel it,
In the warm breeze and sunshine above.

We hold it in our hearts, our souls,
It's my gift to you,
I see it in your smile, your eyes,
So powerful so true.

I'd be lost without it,
I don't know what I'd do
Hope, a small word with huge meaning,
Believe me it's true.

Claire Adamson

from ON FORGETTING THAT I AM A TREE

A poem in which I am growing.

A poem in which I am a tree,
And I am both appreciated and undervalued.

A poem in which I fear I did not dig into the past,
Did not think about my roots,
Forgot what it meant to be planted.

A poem in which I realise they may try to cut
   me down,
That I must change with the seasons,
That I do it so well
It looks like they are changing with me.

A poem in which I remember I have existed
   for centuries,
That centuries are far too small a unit of
   measurement,
That time found itself in the forests, woods
   and jungles.
Remember I have witnessed creation,
That I am key to it.

A poem in which some will carve their names
   into my skin
In hopes the universe will know them.
Where I am so tall I kiss the sun.
Trees cannot hide,
They belong to the day and to the night,
To the past and the future.

A poem in which I stop looking for it,
Because I am home.
I am habitat.
My branches are host and shelter
I am life-giver and fruit-bearer.
Self-sufficient protection.

A poem in which I remember I am a tree.

Ruth Awolola

I AWOKE TO THE CONFUSION
OF A NEW DAY . . .

I awake to the confusion of a new day
The scraps of dreams, memories of yesterday, and new
    cravings creeping into awareness.
The sun spilling its light over all but the shadows and a
    cacophony of sound
From outside and in.
What to make order of? What to let go?
And who makes the choice?
I think I will go down to the river and just watch it flow,
It's been a long time since I have done something really
    important.

David Sluyter

I CHOOSE LOVE

When it turns to dark
And my heart says hide
I can still love.
When I can't inspire
Or feel the muse around me
Still, I can love.
When the air has gone dry
When my throat is muffled
When I can no longer sing
I can still choose love.
When the words fail me
When everything is wrecked
When love has forsaken me
And my memories fade
So that I'm forsaking myself
There is still a space for love.
When my soul fragments
When my joints thicken in fury
When my eyes gloss over
And I can hear the ocean wailing
When the world is torn to bits
I can still love, and love again.
When the magic fades away
When I've lost my perspective
When my protection is gone

And my nerves are shot
When the tears won't stop
When I never want them to
I can always choose love.
When the sky hangs heaviest
When fear is the loudest sound
When I collapse into a pile
And passions run mad
When colours bleed and spill
I can choose the path of love.
When the platform is gone,
When I don't understand
Anything at all about love,
I will still, as best as I can,
Choose love.

Tammy T. Stone

'HOPE' IS THE THING WITH FEATHERS

'Hope' is the thing with feathers –
That perches in the soul –
And sings the tune without the words –
And never stops – at all –

And sweetest – in the Gale – is heard –
And sore must be the storm –
That could abash the little Bird
That kept so many warm –

I've heard it in the chillest land –
And on the strangest Sea –
Yet – never – in Extremity,
It asked a crumb – of me.

Emily Dickinson

III. SETTING OUT
The path of hope

*

from 'NEW EVERY MORNING'

Every day is a fresh beginning;
  Listen, my soul, to the glad refrain,
And, spite of old sorrow and older sinning,
  And puzzles forecasted and possible pain,
  Take heart with the day, and begin again.

Susan Coolidge

We walk from the late morning sunshine into the dark
  musty smell of sleep.

You know the code, the hiding place, I am the senior nurse,
  the teacher, I take your lead.

Mary lies in the hospital bed, a few years from 100. She is
  frail, lost in the covers.

You move towards her, introductions, reassurance.

We know our roles – but not as a performance. We are our
  authentic selves.

Little is spoken between us, two experienced nurses, each
  knowing her part.

You soothe Mary, you play her music. To Patsy Cline I
  begin. Unravelling dressings, preparing skin.

We both work to our rhythm but mainly to Mary's.

We are as one. Both reacting to cues, facial expression,
  flinching, sighs.

You are my eyes and tell me to pause. You hold her hand.
    Make her laugh.

We begin again, you have changed your tack, focusing on
    breathing, stories of her life.

The procedure is done.

You write the notes. I look at you, confident in yourself,
    shining new ideas. Ready for your adventure ahead, my
    role is to get you there.

I think of my qualifications, outdated in the current time
    They mean nothing. It is support, enabling, advice that
    you look to from me. I know my role.

'What do you think?' you ask. I am content.

                         Nicki White

ON NURSES

Surely this is more a calling than a job. The doldrums of the nightshift pierced with the odd life-threatening injury, applying pressure to a gaping wound. Their nurses' shoes clip-clopping down the halls, the thoughts of patients' suffering or dead following them back home. Surely they know that life is random, how death can creep up on the innocent. But how their instincts can sometimes pull spirits back from the brink into their bodies. Like midwives to the spirit. In that moment, do they forget the training and think, if I do this, perhaps they will live? Can you train instinct? I'm not sure. They see it all: the birth, the death, the vomit, the blood, the shock, the diseased, the perturbed, the pain, the smiles. I see them pressing their uniforms for the next shift, washing their hands with soap that makes their palms peel.

Roger Robinson

MAKING A DIFFERENCE
(a poem to be read aloud)

We are shaking and breaking and waking indifference
We are quaking and taking and making a difference

We are working observing recording researching
Wherein we're conferring subverting referring

We're counting the minutes the moments the loss
Redressing the balance addressing the cost

We are citing and fighting it's all in the writing
The spark is igniting in dark we are lightning

We are breaking the brackets the fact is the planet's
In rackets and rackets of rackets in brackets

The systems the victims the damning the scamming
The biased predicting the beating and banning

We teach through closed doors when none listen we hear
When heads turn away we volunteer

To relentless censors the damned and defenceless
Our words are the action the louder reaction

We count the cells in illness we name the unnamed
We count the invisible we make change

We work we stand tall we rise up to be counted
We work above all we climb mountains

The skills we exchange the breaking of chains
The actions sustained the makers of change

We are shaking and breaking and waking indifference
We are quaking and taking and making a difference

Lemn Sissay

LABOUR WARD PRAYER

Give us this day our daily miracle.
Exchange our offering of sweat and tears
and, most of all, blood,
for a new life, crumpled as a new leaf bud.

A child is like a pearl, made of pain
And as we sweat the spiral through again,
There's something holy in this moment now.
The mingled prayers and blasphemies, *I can't, I can't*
become *I can*, become *I must*, because
all life hones down into this single point –

the baby. And here at last she comes –
high perfect cry, eyes closed against the light.
Triumphant, exulting. I wash my hands and leave.
They need me for the miracle next door.

Vicky Thomas

MY BABY BELONGS TO THE HEALTH BOARD

My baby belongs to the Health Board.
I feel like we've got her on loan.
And parents are here by permission
in this baby-processing zone.

They schedule perpetual visits
and set an intractable sum.
I am the square root of my baby.
I do have a name, besides Mum.

They draw me a breastfeeding table.
I don't know what that's all about –
with headwords and columns and so on.
Milk in and then excrement out.

I'm wrecked and depressed and exhausted
and motherhood is an exam.
I stare at the scales as my daughter
first gains and then loses a gram.

I'm only confused by these pamphlets,
'cause none of the diagrams match.
With what magic formula does one
correct a sub-optimal latch?

It might be a bit sore at first, dear,
before it becomes a routine.
There's bruises on my areolae.
What level of sore does she mean?

My baby belongs to the Health Board.
She fell off a centile today.
Forgive me my postnatal terror;
I'm worried they'll take her away.

Nuala Watt

DO LEANABH GUN BHREITH

Cha tusa toradh na dùrachd,
cha tus' an dùil air a coilionadh,
thus' a ghineadh gun aire –
aiteal de dh'aithneachd eadar coigrich.

Tha an t-abhall crom anns a' ghaillinn,
a bhlàth ga shracadh bho na geugan,
an sneachd ga dhinneadh thar na dùthcha,
na cleiteagan gam miuchadh sna cuantan,

A naoidhein, air ar saoghal dèan tròcair,
gabh ort cor min-bhreòite nan daoine
san t-soinninn aoibhinn shàmhaich
tha am broinn do mhàthar a' sgaoileadh.

Meg Bateman

TO AN UNBORN CHILD

Not you the fruit of hope,
not you the fulfilment of promise.
child conceived without thought –
glimmer of recognition between strangers.

The apple tree bends in the storm,
its blossoms torn from the branch,
snow drives across the land,
flakes smothered on the waves.

Child, pity our world,
take on mankind's fair frailty
in the bright joyful calm
that spreads through your mother's womb.

Meg Bateman

WELCOME WEE ONE

O ma darlin wee one
At last you are here in the wurld
And wi' aa your wisdom
Your een bricht as the stars,
You've filled this hoose with licht,
Yer trusty wee huan, your globe o' a heid,
My cherished yin, my hert's ain!

O ma darlin wee one
The hale wurld welcomes ye:
The mune glowes; the hearth wairms.
Let your life hae luck, health, charm,
Ye are my bonny blessed bairn,
My small miraculous gift.
I never kent luve like this.

                                    Jackie Kay

SOUL TO SOUL

Here we are, soul to soul
Heart calling deep to deep
As we journey together to birth this precious new life
Into this welcoming world.

You are not a machine
You are not a spirit trapped in a body.
You are whole . . .
You are one being labouring
To give birth to another.

You are not a machine,
Devoid of
Life history
Connectedness
Relationships
Dignity
You are a whole soul.

And I your soulmate for this time
Labouring with you
Accompanying you in this body marathon
Of pain, resistance and acceptance.

I hold your eyes with mine
Allowing my strength and knowing
My peace and confidence
To settle your fears and pain.

I hold your eyes warmly
Encouraging you in this striving to give new life.

Soul to soul
Heart to heart
Eye wisdom to eye wisdom
We continue together
You are my focus and I am yours

I hold in my hand
The promise of your future
You hold in your being and memory
My authenticity kindness and integrity.

Through the intimacy of this time
We are bonded in
Love, Compassion and Hope.

Clare Alexander

DRIVING TO THE HOSPITAL

We were low on petrol
so I said let's freewheel
when we get to the hill.
It was dawn and the city
was nursing its quiet
and I liked the idea
of arriving with barely
a crunch on the gravel.
You smiled kindly and
eased the clutch gently
and backed us out of
the driveway and patted
my knee with exactly
the gesture you used
when we were courting,
remember, on the way
to your brother's: *I like
driving with my baby,*
that's what you said. And
at the time I wondered
why my heart leapt and leapt.

Kate Clanchy

IV. GRIT AND GRACE

Making sense of pain and death

*

SONNET 2 *from Autumn Sonnets*

If I can let go as trees let go
Their leaves, so casually, one by one;
If I can come to know what they do know,
That fall is the release, the consummation,
Then fear of time and the uncertain fruit
Would not distemper the great lucid skies
This strangest autumn, mellow and a cure.
If I can take the dark, with open eyes
And call it seasonal, not harsh or strange
(For love itself may need a time of sleep)
And, tree like, stand unmoved before the change
Lose what I lose to keep what I keep
The strong root still alive under the snow
Love will endure – if I can let you go.

May Sarton

BIRDS

On Sydney Street, someone's dropped
a paper bird. I can make those.
The crispness of the fold defines the way
it flies. That, and the way you grasp it.
I once sat with a dying child,
filled his room with yellow birds
from folded X-ray paper.
He gave them eyes and coloured spots
across their wings. Retinoblastoma.
For years I dreamt of marker pen
on naked heads, of basements
where hushed beds passed at night,
hung about with fluids, the chill,
the dark, the roaches, the Night Pink's
outdoor cloak, two of us with torches
to check the sick were sleeping.
Some things stay: the way a blackbird
sings through all the gaps in rain,
the pulsing smell of sun on London
pavements, the art of folding paper.

Ann Gray

PRAYER FOR OUR HEALING

When I feel overwhelmed by destruction,
Let me go down to the sea.
Let me sit by the immeasurable ocean
And watch the surf
Beating in and running out all day and all night,
Let me sit by the sea
And have the bitter sea winds
Slap my cheeks with their cold, damp hands
Until I am sensible again.
Let me look at the sky at night
And let the stars tell me
Of limitless horizons and unknown universes
Until I am grown calm and strong once more.

Marjorie Pizer

KINDNESS

To recap what we now know: it did not begin
in a laboratory in Wuhan, nor with a pangolin or bat,
but it already lay dormant within us, like a seed
in need of certain conditions to grow;

its symptoms are many and various,
and may include some, or all, of the following:
tear drops, sudden laughter, a feeling of warmth,
and a peculiar uplifting of the heart;

it leaves its traces everywhere: from boxes
left on doorsteps to conversations over fences;
it can be transmitted over vast distances,
through a phone call, or from a smile across a street,

or a certain softness of tone spoken beside
a hospital bed; it affects young and old equally;
there is no race or gender immune from it;
it has the power to topple bad governments;

if one person were to pass it on to just three others
and they, in turn, were to pass it on to three more,
in no time at all, the world would be full of it,
and where, might we ask ourselves, would we be then.

Brian Bilston

THE PATTERN

Blu-tacked against the window, translucent paper
cut and folded to make a dress
for the young girl who dreams in her hospital bed
in morphine induced sleep.
Saturday is her wedding day; nurses' hands
work against the dark to match the pattern
to white silk with pinned on satin roses.
This bride will be wheeled down corridors

to where she'll make promises. To have and to hold
knowing a life might last a week. Still the chaplain
takes her through her vows. Favourite nurses
will be maids of honour; to carry the intravenous drip,
ensure the wheelchair doesn't catch her dress.

Night bears down upon the ground.
Off-duty nurses gather, smooth, tack and stitch.

Wendy French

YELLOW METAL

An hour dead, his watch is still ticking.
It is the first thing you remove.
Wordless, we start the washing.
Glove-warm suds spreading
ebb tide lines of love.

In the space between the cradle
of your arm and his hollowed temple,
now your words fall gentle,
binding in light
as you wind the sheet circle.

This is nursing, I'm sold.
Then the way you tell me
on the inventory,
that yellow metal is
our watch word, not gold.
No spin. Just grit, and grace.

I'm in.

Colin MacDuff

MY MOTHER DESCRIBES HOW SHE WOULD
WASH THE BODIES

In my country, *she says*, we wash the bodies
three times; they must be family and only women
for the women, and men for the men.

First time with water and plum leaves, second the water
is with kapur and last time purest water; then a bag
with dried rice to close the eyes; a scarf to hold close the
mouth.

When I come to this country, *she says*, in your NHS,
I must to wear stockings and show my legs;
and wash all the bodies; sometimes seven or six together

there in room, and sometime they make tiny movement,
I catch with my eyes an arm falling,
or fingers tighten and the skin is fragile, like paper

and weeping. And then the sighs and the hisses.

On the walk to the nurses' quarters the men watch my legs
in stockings and *Go back to where you came from Paki*
and I tell them, we are headed to same place,

skin same purple and grey
and gently weeping.

Deborah Alma

MY LAST WORDS

'It all adds up to whatever it all adds up to'
Some day suddenly (if I'm lucky)
I'll simply go out like a light
Without time to say anything
Much less deliver
The spontaneous aphorism
I've already drafted
But has yet to be finalised

Frank Ormsby

HIGH FLIGHT

Oh! I have slipped the surly bonds of Earth
And danced the skies on laughter-silvered wings;
Sunward I've climbed, and joined the tumbling mirth
Of sun-split clouds, – and done a hundred things
You have not dreamed of – wheeled and soared and swung
High in the sunlit silence. Hov'ring there,
I've chased the shouting wind along, and flung
My eager craft through footless halls of air . . .

Up, up the long, delirious burning blue
I've topped the wind-swept heights with easy grace
Where never lark, or ever eagle flew –
And, while with silent, lifting mind I've trod
The high untrespassed sanctity of space,
Put out my hand, and touched the face of God.

John Gillespie Magee

WE MOURN YOUR CHILDREN TOO

We mourn your children too.
We do. We cry. We try
to make each touch a loving one –
for short lives should be full of love.
We cry. We do. We try
to keep our grief walled up, not stealing yours.
To meet your eyes steadily.
To find the joy wherever it can fall.
We cry. We try. We do.
We're honoured when we help you say goodbye.
The farewells break us too;
the cracks are how the light gets out.
You hate us, love us, hug us, blame us.
You wonder how we do it.
So do we. We try. We cry.
We mourn your children too.

                    Vicky Thomas

V. STILL WE RISE

Finding our voices and being the change

*

STILL I RISE

You may write me down in history
With your bitter, twisted lies,
You may tread me in the very dirt
But still, like dust, I'll rise.

Does my sassiness upset you?
Why are you beset with gloom?
'Cause I walk like I've got oil wells
Pumping in my living room.

Just like moons and like suns,
With the certainty of tides,
Just like hopes springing high,
Still I'll rise.

Did you want to see me broken?
Bowed head and lowered eyes?
Shoulders falling down like teardrops.
Weakened by my soulful cries.

Does my haughtiness offend you?
Don't you take it awful hard
'Cause I laugh like I've got gold mines
Diggin' in my own back yard.

You may shoot me with your words,
You may cut me with your eyes,
You may kill me with your hatefulness,
But still, like air, I'll rise.

Does my sexiness upset you?
Does it come as a surprise
That I dance like I've got diamonds
At the meeting of my thighs?

Out of the huts of history's shame
I rise
Up from a past that's rooted in pain
I rise
I'm a black ocean, leaping and wide,
Welling and swelling I bear in the tide.
Leaving behind nights of terror and fear
I rise
Into a daybreak that's wondrously clear
I rise
Bringing the gifts that my ancestors gave,
I am the dream and the hope of the slave.
I rise
I rise
I rise.

                              Maya Angelou

THE DOOR

Go and open the door.
    Maybe outside there's
    a tree, or a wood,
    a garden,
    or a magic city.

Go and open the door.
    Maybe a dog's rummaging.
    Maybe you'll see a face,
or an eye,
or the picture
    of a picture.

Go and open the door.
    If there's a fog
    it will clear.

Go and open the door.
    Even if there's only
    the darkness ticking,
    even if there's only
    the hollow wind,

even if
   nothing
      is there,
go and open the door.

At least
there'll be
a draught.

Miroslav Holub
Translated from Czech by
Iain Milner

A CENTER

You must hold your quiet center,
where you do what only you can do.
If others call you a maniac or a fool,
just let them wag their tongues.
If some praise your perseverance,
don't feel too happy about it –
only solitude is a lasting friend.

You must hold your distant center.
Don't move even if earth and heaven quake.
If others think you are insignificant,
that's because you haven't held on long enough.
As long as you stay put year after year,
eventually you will find a world
beginning to revolve around you.

Ha Jin

HOW TO BEHAVE WITH THE ILL

Approach us assertively, try not to
cringe or sidle, it makes us fearful.
Rather walk straight up and smile.
Do not touch us unless invited,
particularly don't squeeze upper arms,
or try to hold our hands. Keep your head erect.
Don't bend down, or lower your voice.
Speak evenly. Don't say
'How are you?' in an underlined voice.
Don't say, 'I heard that you were very ill'.
This makes the poorly paranoid.
Be direct, say 'How's your cancer?'
Try not to say how well we look.
compared to when you met in Safeway's.
Please don't cry, or get emotional,
and say how dreadful it all is.
Also (and this is hard I know)
try not to ignore the ill, or to scurry
past, muttering about a bus, the bank.
Remember that this day might be your last
and that it is a miracle that any of us
stands up, breathes, behaves at all.

Julia Darling

THE WAY I SEE IT
(to be read both ways)

Everything's going to be okay
So don't try to tell me that
I'm dying
Because right now
My life is full of hope
You cannot convince me
That time is getting short
I can see clearly
My future is all planned out

Rachel McCoubrie

NIGHT TALK

He speaks of death – his death, how parts
of him have died. It's midnight,
he's on my computer screen, grey metal limbs
in trainers, no socks under green trousers.

He has half a right arm, a large left hand,
three rings on his little finger, a creased forehead,
a rounded mouth as he tells his story
about a snowball that saved his life:

one the hospice nurse brought to his bed,
made him catch, crunch, feel the chill,
one that made him laugh again –
the dust of snow in white-blue air.

                    Audrey Ardern-Jones

LEAVING EARLY

My Love,
  tonight Fionnuala is your nurse.
You'll hear her voice sing-song around the ward
lifting a wing at the shore of your darkness.
I heard that, in another life, she too journeyed
through a storm, a kind of curse, with the ocean
rising darkly around her, fierce with cold,
and no resting place, only the frozen
rocks that tore her feet, the light on her shoulders.

And no cure there but to wait it out.
If, while I'm gone, your fever comes down –
if the small, salt-laden shapes of her song
appear to you as a first glimmer of earth-light,
follow the sweet, hopeful voice of that landing.
She will keep you safe beneath her wing.

                    Leanne O'Sullivan

GRACE

That year we danced to green bleeps on screen.
My son had come early, just the 1kg of him,
all big head, bulging eyes and blue veins.

On the ward I met Grace. A Jamaican senior nurse
who sang pop songs on her shift, like they were hymns.
'Your son feisty. Y'see him ah just pull off the breathing mask.'

People spoke of her in half tones down these carbolic halls.
Even the doctors gave way to her, when it comes
to putting a line into my son's nylon thread of a vein.

She'd warn junior doctors with trembling hands: 'Me only letting you
                try twice.'
On her night shift she pulls my son's incubator into her room,
no matter the tangled confusion of wires and machine.

When the consultant told my wife and I on morning rounds
that he's not sure my son will live, and if he lives he might never
                leave the hospital,
she pulled us quickly aside: 'Him have no right to say that
                – just raw so.'

Another consultant tells the nurses to stop feeding a baby,
          who will soon die,
and she commands her loyal nurses to feed him. 'No baby must dead
wid a hungry belly.' And she'd sit in the dark, rocking that
          well-fed baby,

held to her bosom, slowly humming the melody of 'Happy' by Pharrell.
And I think, if by some chance, I'm not here and my son's life
          should flicker,
then Grace, she should be the one.

                    Roger Robinson

THE DRIVE HOME

After a nightshift
At 7 a.m.

In the hyperbaric oxygen chamber
Of your shiny car

Rain draining off the windscreen
As you are lifted
Into daylight

You think the paparazzi
Should be here

Because once again
You failed

No
Just your cold bed

Your conscience

Craig Coyle

TRY TO PRAISE THE MUTILATED WORLD

Try to praise the mutilated world.
Remember June's long days,
and wild strawberries, drops of rosé wine.
The nettles that methodically overgrow
the abandoned homesteads of exiles.
You must praise the mutilated world.
You watched the stylish yachts and ships;
one of them had a long trip ahead of it,
while salty oblivion awaited others.
You've seen the refugees going nowhere,
you've heard the executioners sing joyfully.
You should praise the mutilated world.
Remember the moments when we were together
in a white room and the curtain fluttered.
Return in thought to the concert where music flared.
You gathered acorns in the park in autumn
and leaves eddied over the earth's scars.
Praise the mutilated world
and the gray feather a thrush lost,
and the gentle light that strays and vanishes
and returns.

Adam Zagajewski
Translated by Clare Cavanagh

CT SCANNER

This is where we come
to let ourselves be seen.
This is where we meet
our truth transected.

This is where we stay
while others leave the room:
the vein found
the dye injected.

'Breathe in and hold your breath'

This is when the bed
slips us in then out,
the scanner smoothly reading
our body's passing barcode.

This is where we lie
still as Schrödinger's cat,
holding our breath
innocent of outcome.

This is when we know
that we truly do not know
the images now moving
in front of expert eyes.

We find ourselves
– lost in translation.

This is where we dress
our bodies and our fears
in well-kent clothes
and walk our way back home.

And this is where we know –
    our arms are held
    our hearts are warmed
    and our spirits steadied
by sure hands, clear eyes and kindly chat.

We find ourselves
– lost in gratitude.

Mary Gunn

SOLIDARITY POEM

Did we imagine life would find us like this,
lead us here like this?
Did we not think we would be the ones to find it?
Will we be the ones to resist attacks on equality, dignity,
    fairness, autonomy, respect –
two world wars were required for people
to form a formal idea that these ideals belong to all.
A post-war dream to keep the seams of humanity intact.
Now the ambush on those intrinsic values is on,
and you are the battlefield front line
armed with expectations of decency
articulations of suffering, asking questions to barrels of
    eclipsed guns –
when your time on this earth is gone,
what would you like to have done?
The guns may stay silent,
but you will not
and because of that, because of you,
we can still hold the hand of a child,
talk to them quietly about the goodness of hearts

people's ability to learn from the past
to become kinder
to be the reminder to rules
that human rights are for us all.

Sabrina Mahfouz

BEANNACHT / BLESSING

for Josie, my mother

On the day when
the weight deadens
on your shoulders
and you stumble,
may the clay dance
to balance you.

And when your eyes
freeze behind
the grey window
and the ghost of loss
gets into you,
may a flock of colours,
indigo, red, green
and azure blue,
come to awaken in you
a meadow of delight.

When the canvas frays
in the currach of thought
and a stain of ocean

blackens beneath you,
may there come across the waters
a path of yellow moonlight
to bring you safely home.

May the nourishment of the earth be yours,
may the clarity of light be yours,
may the fluency of the ocean be yours,
may the protection of the ancestors be yours.

And so may a slow
wind work these words
of love around you,
an invisible cloak
to mind your life.

John O'Donohue

SPACE FOR REFLECTION

*

*We invite you to use this space for scribbling your own thoughts /
poems / reflections and to take some time for yourself:*

ACKNOWLEDGEMENTS

Our thanks are due to the following authors, publishers, and estates who have generously given permission to reproduce works. We have endeavoured to contact and clear permissions with all poets and publishers listed here; if there are any omissions, please contact the Scottish Poetry Library.

Claire Adamson, 'All Around Us' by permission of the author; Deborah Alma, 'My Mother Describes How She Would Wash the Bodies' by permission of the author and first published in *These Are The Hands: Poems from the Heart of the NHS*, co-edited by Deborah Alma and Dr Katie Amiel, with all profits going to NHS Charities Together (Fair Acre Press, 2020); Maya Angelou, 'Still I Rise' from *And Still I Rise: A Book of Poems*. Copyright © 1978 by Maya Angelou. Used by permission of Random House, an imprint and division of Penguin Random House LLC. All rights reserved; Audrey Ardern-Jones, 'Night Talk' from *Doing the Rounds* (Indigo Dreams Publishing, 2019), by permission of the publisher; Ruth Awolola, from 'On Forgetting That I am a Tree' from *Rising Stars: New Young Voices in Poetry* (Otter-Barry Books); Meg Bateman, 'Do Leanabh Gun Bhreith /

Together (Fair Acre Press, 2020); Rachel McCoubrie, 'The Way I See It' by permission of the author and first published in *These Are The Hands: Poems from the Heart of the NHS*, co-edited by Deborah Alma and Dr Katie Amiel, with all profits going to NHS Charities Together (Fair Acre Press, 2020); John O' Donohue, 'Beannacht/Blessing' from *Echoes of Memory* (Transworld Publishing, 2010) by permission of the author's estate and 'Time to be Slow' from *To Bless the Space Between Us* (Random House, 2008); Frank Ormsby, 'My Last Words' from *The Darkness of Snow* (Bloodaxe, 2017), reprinted by permission of the publisher; Leanne O'Sullivan, 'Leaving Early' from *A Quarter of an Hour* (Bloodaxe, 2018), reprinted by permission of the publisher; Marjorie Pizer, 'Prayer for our Healing' from *To You the Living: Poems of Bereavement and Loss*; Roger Robinson, 'Grace' and 'On Nurses' from *A Portable Paradise* (Peepal Tree Press, 2020); Jelaluddin Rumi, trans. Coleman Barks, 'The Guest House', from *Rumi: Selected Poems*, trans. Coleman Barks with John Moynce, A. J. Arberry, Reynold Nicholson (Penguin Books, 2004), by permission of Penguin Books Ltd; May Sarton, 'Sonnet 2' from *Collected Poems, 1930-1993*, W. W. Norton & Company 1992. Used by permission of the publishers. Lemn Sissay, 'Making A Difference' by permission of the author, written in role as Chancellor of Manchester University, and published in *These Are The Hands: Poems from the Heart of the NHS*, co-edited by Deborah Alma and Dr Katie Amiel, with all profits going to NHS Charities Together (Fair Acre Press, 2020) and 'Rest' © Lemn Sissay, 2016 from *Gold From the Stone: New and Selected Poems*, reproduced by permission of Canongate Books Ltd.; David Sluyter, 'I awoke to the confusion of a new day . . .' Fetzer Institute, Michigan from *Prayers for a Thousand Years* by Elizabeth Roberts, Elias Amidon. Copyright © 1999 by Elizabeth Roberts and Elias Amidon. Used by permission of HarperCollins Publishers; Tammy Stone Takahashi, 'I Choose Love' by permission of the author and first published on Journey of the Heart (womenspiritualpoetry.blogspot.com); Vicky Thomas, 'We mourn your children too' and 'Labour Ward Prayer' by permission of the author and first published in *These Are The Hands: Poems from the Heart of the NHS*, co-edited by Deborah Alma and Dr Katie Amiel, with all profits going to NHS Charities Together (Fair Acre Press, 2020); Nuala Watt, 'My Baby Belongs to the Health Board' by permission of the author; Nicki White, 'The Meet Visit' by permission of the author; Adam Zagajewski, 'Try to Praise the Mutilated World' from *Without End: New and Selected Poems* © 2002 by Adam Zagajewski. Used by permission of Farrar, Straus & Giroux, LLC, http://us.macmillan.com/fsg.